The 40 Day Way

40 Days of Devotionals to Challenge, Strengthen,
and Develop your Walk with God

Lawrence Trimble

STRONG
PUBLISHING
HOUSE

Bringing the strength of your words to reality

Lawrence Trimble

The 40 Day Way

40 Days of Devotionals to Challenge, Strengthen, and Develop your Walk with God

The 40 Day Way Revised 2nd Edition
*40 Days of Devotionals to Challenge, Strengthen, and
Develop your Walk with God*

Published by Strong Publishing House
Inquiries: strongpublishinghouse@gmail.com
Website: strongpublishinghouse.weebly.com

<u>Contents</u>

Acknowledgments

I first and foremost want to thank my Lord and Savior Jesus Christ for saving me and giving me the ability to touch many lives through ministry, and the gift of writing. Without Him I cannot be me.

To the love of my life my wife Brittanie, thank you for being there for me, encouraging me, and being my motivation.

To my three sons Lawrence Jr., Brayden, and Canaan, my armourbearers, Daddy loves you.

To my mother Annette (RIP), I love you for giving me life in the natural realm and raising me to be the man I have become. To my parents, Uncle Chubby and Aunt Linda, I love you and thank you for instilling the passion to live saved, even when I didn't want to hear it.

To my sister and brothers: Adrienne, Jermaine, and Vince love you all. To all my family, friends, and loved ones: I cannot name all of you one by one, but I appreciate you, and Love you dearly.

To Apostle William and Prophetess Donna Rogers, thank you for your continual spiritual guidance. To Overseer and Sister Walker thank you for covering me and Britt in the beginning phases of ministry.

To Drs. Johnny and Pamela Drumgole, thank you for showing me how to walk out my life with Jesus Christ at a young age.

To mentor Fred Minner your guidance and mentorship has been greatly appreciated, and you have gone above and beyond.

To the Body of Christ, remain in the battle, fighting the good fight of faith.

To all those who helped this vision become a reality. Spiritual advisors, editors, reviewers, supporters, I appreciate you and thank you dearly!!!

~ Lawrence

How to use this book

The 40 Day Way is designed to equip Christians with scriptures to engrain and implement in their daily life. Research shows it takes 21 days to develop a consistent process; The 40 Day Way uses this same systematic theory to develop a consistent process of implementing God's Word into the spirit of believers. Here are some useful tips in utilizing this supplemental tool:

- Use this book one day at a time as a supplemental tool. You do not have to read like a novel.
- Make sure to pray after reading.
- Commit a time of devotion to God and stick to it as much as possible. Your daily time can be morning, afternoon, or evening.
- Most important ask God for revelation knowledge.
- Record notes of God's blessings and personal insights.
- Search for other scriptures centered on the topic read during your devotional time.
- After completing the 40 days, continue a strategy to read scriptures and pray as you are now building your spiritual man.

IN THE MIDST OF THE WILDERNESS

Mark 1:12-13, NKJV
12 Immediately the Spirit drove Him into the wilderness.
13 And He was there in the wilderness forty days, tempted by
Satan, and was with the wild beasts; and the angels ministered
to Him.

There are key situations that our Father allows us to go through to test our faith and mature us spiritually. We are pushed to endure these times in our lives to develop our Spiritual walk with him, and obtain a better understanding of what he requires of us while walking with him. A good example to follow is Jesus being led into the wilderness to be tested by Satan. For 40 days he was tested in three different areas of life: Lust of the flesh (turning stones to bread), lust of the eyes (kingdoms of this world), and pride of life (making angels move to his command). Jesus overcomes these temptations by speaking the Word of the Lord and defeating the attack of the enemy. As a believer, your understanding and knowledge of God's Word is imperative in order to properly apply in daily living. Satan comes to challenge your walk with God, attempting to get your flesh, eyes, and desires away from God's purpose for your life. The Word of God must be engrained in your Spirit, ensuring you will overcome obstacles and progress at a consistent pace in the Kingdom of God.

As Jesus entered the wilderness, the Bible states the Holy Spirit led him there. Believers will enter wilderness-type experiences through our natural environment. The wilderness represents a place of uncertainty, chaos, rebellion, strife, jealousy, depression, lack of faith, doubt, unbelief, disorganization, limited visibility, unorthodoxy, and materialistic indulgence where our faith and trust in God is tried. Similarly, our wilderness experience can encourage the desire to become unnatural, self-gratifying, materialistic, and heretical. Additionally, as Jesus was led into the wilderness to be tempted, we are allowed to be tempted by Satan. Therefore, it is essential that our relationship with God be built on His word as the foundation and final authority. In the midst of the wilderness, Jesus was tested, he spoke the living Word of the Lord, and God's angels took care of him. For this similar effect in our individual lives, we must position ourselves to speak the Word of the Lord over all of our situations; and know God's angels have charge over us and will take care of us.

Be Blessed,

Minister Lawrence Trimble

SECTION 1

TRAINING:
WELCOME TO YOUR NEW JOURNEY

Day One

Romans 6:14-15, KJV

14 For sin shall not have dominion over you: for ye are not under the law, but under grace. 15 What then? shall we sin, because we are not under the law, but under grace? God forbid.

For a Christian, it is important to understand, that the mind has to be retrained on a daily basis. Man's old sinful nature includes participation and indulgence in behaviors that provide convenience to the flesh; which results in a habitual response to being gratified and satisfied in sin. Our old sinful nature produces sinful habits and results, which could be considered normal if not properly redirected. Christ's manifestation brought light to every sinful place of life; and provides the redirection and retraining of our thinking to line up with the Word of God. This thinking creates freedom through the grace of God received by faith in Jesus. Sin is bondage in the flesh. A daily retraining of our thinking should line up with God's word, so we will be free from sin's bondage.

Father, I thank you that you have released me from the grip and tyranny of sin. Teach me your ways. Let my thoughts and actions line up with your will for my life. It is my desire to continue to please you. If any situation arises to produce a negative response from my old nature, I pray that you give wisdom and guidance through your Holy Spirit that I will not fall for Satan's devices. I bless you now for true freedom through Jesus Christ my Savior. In Jesus' Name Amen

Day Two

John 4:13-14, KJV

13 Jesus answered and said unto her, Whosoever drinketh of this water shall thirst again: 14 But whosoever drinketh of the water that I shall give him shall never thirst ; but the water that I shall give him shall be in him a well of water springing up into everlasting life.

After one has been satisfied, the body's response of fulfillment remains until it has absorbed all it can from what satisfied it in the beginning. Subsequently, the body's desire for fulfillment leads it to search for an equivalent satisfaction. In the natural realm, this response happens frequently to satisfy the basic necessities of life. It is imperative to have a spiritually intense desire to fulfill the needs of our spirit. As we drink from the well of living water, through a disciplined lifestyle, our spirit becomes stronger and edified. Ultimately the results are believers who are more in tuned to the Holy Spirit, who is the guide of all their actions.

Father, My desire is to receive this water in which I will never have to thirst again. Allow me to develop a disciplined lifestyle where my desire is connected to your desire, and my actions are in line with your actions. My soul longs to be where your spirit is. My spirit does not want to be dried out from the lack of living water, which you desire for your people to partake in. I pray as I walk with you enlighten my way and my desire to line up with your ways so that I will receive eternal life. In Jesus' Name, Amen

Day Three

Galatians 5:16, KJV

16 This I say then, Walk in the Spirit, and ye shall not fulfill the lust of the flesh.

The development of a Christ-like lifestyle (living inside the will of God) is the beginning stages of a transition of ideas, beliefs, morals, values, and overall thinking. This transition creates a new person, who is changed by the driving force (Holy Spirit) behind him. The aspiration to live by the Spirit takes the place of the tendency to live by the selfish desires or wants in each individual. Individualization is good and much needed, furthermore, the expression of that individualization should be well-maintained and within the appropriate guidelines. These guidelines are the motivation to begin to transform an individual into the spiritual being he or she desires to become. When we realize the Spirit is higher than the self, we will become motivated to walk by the Christ-like lifestyle (living inside the will of God), and use the Word of God as our guideline.

Father, Teach me to walk according to your spirit. I know that I am nothing without you, but with you I am everything you desire for me to become. My purpose is not to allow my personal desires to overshadow what you are attempting to do in my life. Your spirit and your will are the most important attributes I can have. So, as I walk with you, continue to illuminate my pathway with your Spirit. Continue to show me the true direction I need to go. I choose to walk according to your Word, in the Spirit of Truth. In Jesus' Name, Amen

Day Four

Titus 2:7, 8, NIV

7 In everything set them an example by doing what is good. In your teaching show integrity, seriousness 8 and soundness of speech that cannot be condemned, so that those who oppose you may be ashamed because they have nothing bad to say about us.

Integrity and maturity guide our daily actions. They guide us in becoming like Christ by paying close attention to His principles. Living a life of integrity and maturity provides others to see the Christ-like example before them through our lives.

Father, I need to be able to walk in integrity according to the principles of your Word. Teach me continually so that I will not let down the standard. Let good things flow from me like a river, making me an example in the Body of Christ and the world. Allow my life to not be criticized, but celebrated because I represent you. In Jesus' Name, Amen

Day Five

Psalms 1:1-2, KJV

1Blessed is the man that walketh not in the counsel of the ungodly, nor standeth in the way of sinners, nor sitteth in the seat of the scornful. 2 But his delight is in the law of the LORD; and in his law doth he meditate day and night.

The result of following wisdom and instruction is living blessed. In essence, a person who is a follower of sound principles is one who enjoys a happy lifestyle. When we delight in God, God gives the feeling of joy which produces a confidence in what we believe. Avoiding unscriptural, unwise advice is essential to a believer's foundational walk with Christ. Dedicated time and attention should be given to the truths of God and how we implement those truths in our lives.

Father, Let my days be filled with the desire to become more like you. Teach me how to avoid all of the traps and snares that could cause my walk with you to end detrimentally. Teach me to walk as you walk, talk as you talk, become as you are. My joy is satisfied when your joy is fulfilled. Show me how to dedicate my time to serving you. In Jesus' Name, Amen

Day Six

Psalms 7:17, KJV

17 I will praise the LORD according to his righteousness: and will sing praise to the name of the LORD most high.

P riority is defined as something which comes before another either in time, rank, order, precedence, or even privilege. A Christian's walk with God needs to be one of thanksgiving as a priority because of who He is. The very nature of God provokes the need to give him what he deserves: praise, honor, and worship. He becomes priority number 1 in the lives of those who are dedicated to His cause, and illuminated by His truths. As we make God a priority, He makes us a priority.

Father, You continually do more than I can even imagine here on earth. Your pure and perfect state of being is a quality I seek to mimic. Because you are perfect and just, you are worthy of the accolades from my Spirit. Praise is what my soul and spirit will do toward you all the days of my life. You are the one true and living God; therefore, you are worthy to receive all the recognition because you never fail. God I praise you for your nature and character! In Jesus' Name, Amen

Day Seven

Ephesians 6:18-19, KJV

18 Praying always with all prayer and supplication in the Spirit, and watching thereunto with all perseverance and supplication for all saints; 19 And for me, that utterance may be given unto me, that I may open my mouth boldly , to make known the mystery of the gospel,

Communication with God by praying is of the upmost importance. It is a weapon that penetrates not only the camp of the enemy, but it allows us to come before the throne room of God for assistance. Prayer strengthens our relationship with God and develops a sensitive ear to the Holy Spirit's guidance. Not only do we pray, we pray without ceasing, and with an expectation of our prayers being answered. When we are in relationship with God our prayers are necessary to maintain a healthy spiritual balance.

Father, I thank you now for the ability to know how to pray. As you taught your disciples in times past how to pray, I thank you for teaching me how to pray. I know that I must stay in communication with you concerning different situations I encounter on a daily basis, and with that my prayers must be daily. Father, as I pray, teach me your word so I have understanding and wisdom. Let me know the plans and purposes that you have for your people in this life, that we all might grow and mature in your grace. In Jesus Name, Amen

Day Eight

Matthew 5:6, KJV
6 Blessed are they which do hunger and thirst after righteousness: for they shall be filled.

The desire to be filled creates an appetite. Areas lacking necessities desire to be filled and satisfied. As we mature in knowing and living out God's word, our spirit desires to maintain a place of satisfaction. Daily administration of the necessary spiritual food ensures our spiritual appetite will remain satisfied removing spiritual immaturity. When one is satisfied, he becomes energized to accomplish tasks without exhaustion. Our lives should include a daily repetition of administering God's Word to our spirit like the consumption of a daily vitamin.

Father, Your word is my necessary food by which my Spirit expects to be fed. I have tasted of your goodness and this has developed a continuous appetite for your Word. My desire is to seek after your face daily. My prayer is to dive into your word so I will be immersed. As I am immersed, there will always be the desire to maintain the same level of satisfaction, so allow me to be satisfied by your Spirit. In Jesus' Name, Amen

9

Day Nine

Luke 6:12, KJV

12And it came to pass in those days, that he went out into a mountain to pray, and continued all night in prayer to God.

One of the greatest aspects of a relationship is alone, intimate time (Taking Intimate Moments Easy) with one another. It is important that this time is not hindered because it develops and strengthens the relationship beyond the norm, providing a foundation of trust and dependency. Prayer is a driving force of strengthening our relationship with God, and assists in building our spiritual foundation. Without alone time in prayer and studying God's Word, our dependency shifts outside the relationship leading to a weak spiritual foundation. With alone time in prayer and study, our dependency stays within the relationship and a strong foundation is laid. Prayer and study of the word is the glue of intimacy binding all Christians together with God.

Father, Show me the appropriate way to discipline my life by having communion with you daily. I understand that prayer is the best way to maintain communication with you. Prayer is the glue that holds our relationship together, so teach me how to consistently be intimate with you. My desire is not to look to others for my answers, but to look to you. Allow me to trust you for everything, never let me turn my heart away from you. In Jesus' Name, Amen

Day Ten

Jeremiah 3:14, 15 KJV

14 Turn, O backsliding children, saith the LORD; for I am married unto you: and I will take you one of a city, and two of a family, and I will bring you to Zion: 15 And I will give you pastors according to mine heart, which shall feed you with knowledge and understanding.

Covenant relationships establish an everlasting connection with another person. Consistency and dedication are important in covenant relationships, as it allows for the establishment of sound principles. At the heart of the matter we must give our time and attention to cultivating our spirits under the teachings of **Godly** pastors. Pastors who are led by God's spirit show believers how to establish their spiritual walk on the principles of Christ. This covenant relationship is strengthened due to an individual's understanding of scripture is grasped, knowledge can be used, and mistakes avoided.

Father, In order for me to be in complete covenant relationship with you, there is a need for me to understand how to walk according to your purpose. Teach me your ways O God, so I will not walk contrary to your Word. Allow me to understand the truth, and direct me to leaders who teach your truths. Let my soul be satisfied according to the everlasting relationship you have with me. In Jesus' Name, Amen

11

SECTION 2

CONDITIONING: MIND OVER MATTER

Day One

Philippians 2:5-8, KJV

5Let this mind be in you, which was also in Christ Jesus: 6 Who, being in the form of God, thought it not robbery to be equal with God: 7But made himself of no reputation, and took upon him the form of a servant, and was made in the likeness of men: 8 And being found in fashion as a man, he humbled himself, and became obedient unto death, even the death of the cross.

A transition of mindset leads to a transition of actions and beliefs. For one to become solidified in their actions and beliefs there must be a paralleled shift of mindset. The Christian does not desire status and position, but they are identified by humility, sacrifice, and obedience. Although one might obtain a position due to their humble nature, sacrifice of self, and obedience, the focus should not be on achieving a higher status. Throughout your Christian life maintain the desire to remain humble.

Father, As I walk in your word allow me to walk with the spirit of humility. Don't let haughtiness, pride, self-exaltation, or anything get in the way of my being pleasing in your sight. Even if your desire is to bless my life, show me how to accept it and remain humble. My life is not to glorify myself, but to make sure I glorify you. Show me how to live obediently according to your Word. In Jesus' Name, Amen

Day Two

Hosea 6:3, KJV

3 Then shall we know, if we follow on to know the LORD: his going forth is prepared as the morning; and he shall come unto us as the rain, as the latter and former rain unto the earth.

Understanding---The zeal and intensity of our Christian walk should be based on having an understanding of the Word of God. Understanding comes from the knowledge gained by studying the nature and characteristics of the Sovereignty of God, and allowing the Holy Spirit to direct our actions from the word we receive. Without a pure understanding, one will not progress. Seeking to develop a spiritual lifestyle with an understanding of the character, principles, and authority of God is the first essential priority in daily Christian living.

Father, Today I will seek to understand your ways. I cannot do anything without understanding who you are first, then I can understand how I am to become who you have destined me to be. Your direction gives me the proper pathway to your overall desire for me. Allow my mind to be driven to seek out the will of the Lord for my life. Show me your truths, teach me to understand your principles. In Jesus' Name, Amen

Day Three

Daniel 3:18, KJV

18 But if not, be it known unto thee, O king, that we will not serve thy gods, nor worship the golden image which thou hast set up.

Conviction is the assurance of something being true or false. It is the driving force behind the development of one's actions. Without it (conviction), the foundation of a person's values becomes a collection of opposing opinions. The solid basis of the morals and values of a person should be rooted by their conviction. It prevents swaying, changing stances, and choosing opposing decisions. A person's spiritual foundation will not be destroyed when their conviction is based on the truth and strength of God's Word. Make sure your convictional foundation is strong.

Father, I understand that I cannot serve any other God but you. I rest in the assurance that you are my Lord who sent His son so I might have an abundant life. Even in the midst of adverse situations, my conviction is solidified by this truth. I thank you, Lord, for providing me with the everlasting strength to endure harsh times and wonderful times. My foundation is in you. In Jesus' Name, Amen

Day Four

Psalms 118:8-9, KJV

8 It is better to trust in the LORD than to put confidence in man. 9 It is better to trust in the LORD than to put confidence in princes.

Sustainability is key to any relationship one enters into. One should have confidence that the relationship has the capability of enduring tests of hardship without being terminated. Our relationship with our Heavenly Father should be built on a foundation which allows for sustainability. The frailty and unpredictability of human relationships is not where our complete trust should lie. Any Christian relationship built with their ultimate trust in Jesus Christ produces the formula of a relationship that is sustainable.

Father, Allow me to have complete trust in you and your word. My entering into this relationship with you was not for temporary times, but for permanent times. Show me how not to totally rely on natural relationships to maintain satisfaction, but show me how to totally rely on my relationship with you to maintain satisfaction. My prayer is for my covenant relationship to be long-lasting and sustainable. In Jesus' Name, Amen

Day Five

Exodus 3:11, KJV

11 And Moses said unto God, Who am I, that I should go unto Pharaoh, and that I should bring forth the children of Israel out of Egypt?

How Christians evaluate themselves determines their success. The lower placement on an esteem scale results in lower performance; similarly, the higher placement on an esteem scale results in higher performance. As each Christian develops his walk with God, his confidence increases as God transforms him. Negative self-image should always take a rear placement to positive self-image. Continuing to pursue confidence in God through the knowledge of His word provides a Christian with high self-esteem and positive self-image.

Father, As I walk with you, show me who you have created me to be. I will always take authority over any negative thoughts and words which try to devalue who you are molding me to become. The image I have of myself will replicate the image you have for me. As my confidence builds, I will be sure to walk in the things you desire. Today I choose to develop a lifestyle of positive words and positive self-image. In Jesus' Name, Amen

Day Six

Hebrews 12:1-2, NIV

1 Therefore, since we are surrounded by such a great cloud of witnesses, let us throw off everything that hinders and the sin that so easily entangles, and let us run with perseverance the race marked out for us. 2 Let us fix our eyes on Jesus, the author and perfecter of our faith, who for the joy set before him endured the cross, scorning its shame, and sat down at the right hand of the throne of God.

Determination is a key ingredient in the recipe of success in God's purpose. Our determination drives us to endure obstacles, hardships, negativity, sin, dead weight, and challenges with the purpose of overcoming them. Utilizing the examples of those who go before us allows us to accomplish feats at a greater magnitude. As we endeavor to complete our developmental process, we must utilize the examples and accomplishments of our Savior Jesus Christ as a reference of the determination we must have in our personal walk with God.

Father, In the name of Jesus, allow me to keep my focus on you. I will not become sidetracked by the many different obstacles of life along the way. Allow me to make your example of righteousness become the central focus of my spiritual development. This way I can run the race in confidence knowing that the pathway I am taking is one which leads to completion of the course. Thank you, Lord, for being the perfect example of holiness before me, so that I might live as you live. In Jesus' Name, Amen

Day Seven

Ephesians 6: 10, KJV

10 Finally, my brethren, be strong in the Lord, and in the power of his might.

The characteristics of God are identical to His nature. When Christians understand God's characteristics, God's nature can be understood. As we mature in our personal walk with God we should exhibit His nature and characteristics. Everyone we encounter should identify with our characteristics being in alignment with God's characteristics. Strength encompasses all believers' walk of faith as we develop our relationship on spiritual principles. When we walk with God, His strength becomes our strength---and with that strength an immovable foundation materializes.

Father, In you there is everlasting strength that I need to become sound in the faith. Show me the proper spiritual calisthenics which develop the proper lifestyle of faith in you. When phases of life come to make me weak, allow me to experience spiritual rejuvenation and restoration to build me up completely in you. Show me how to overcome any weakness of mind, heart, soul, or spirit that tries to prevent me from being the replication of Christ walking the earth. Strength and power are the characteristics my spirit needs and longs for. In Jesus' Name, Amen

19

Day Eight

Jude 1:20, NIV

20 But you, dear friends, build yourselves up in your most holy faith and pray in the Holy Spirit

How pleasant it is to know that your prayers are directed by the Holy Spirit!!! As Christians are guided by the Holy Spirit, their foundation continues to be strengthened by God's affirmation of His Word. Our prayers become like a GPS *(Guided Prayers (for) Solutions)* for any direction we need in any area of our life. Moreover, as we follow those directions we become confident in our foundational beliefs. Use your GPS *(Guided Prayers (for) Solution*s)!!!

Heavenly Father, My prayer is that you continually guide me according to your spirit. Without your spiritual guidance I am more prone to make mistakes, which is not my desire. With your spiritual guidance I can continually lead a prosperous and successful life. So God, when I pray let my prayers originate from a solid spiritual foundation of faith in you. Let my prayers guide my life, so I can find the solutions to all my needs in life. In Jesus' Name, Amen

Day Nine

1 Corinthians 14:33, KJV

33 For God is not the author of confusion, but of peace, as in all churches of the saints.

The overall goal of every Christian is to have a complete and orderly life. From personal relationships, to finances, to personal character and integrity, and to theoretical mindsets, the goal is order. Our Heavenly Father does not find satisfaction in disorder and chaos. He finds satisfaction in peace, as an attribute of our Heavenly armor (Ephesians 6:15). Peace brings stability as we become ministers of God's grace. As our Christian journey matures, we should continually strive to walk in peace will all men.

Father, My understanding is focused on developing a lifestyle of walking in peace with all I come in contact with. I know that you are walking with me to mature and develop my relationship with you; therefore, I need your grace to assist me in this process. Show me how to avoid discord, strife, unforgiveness, hatred, envy, or any other attribute contrary to your word. My need and desire is to live a peaceful life in the fruitfulness of your word covering me and showing me the direct way to eternal peace and joy. In Jesus' Name, Amen

Day Ten

2 Corinthians 5:20a, KJV
20 Now then we are ambassadors for Christ...

The selection of representatives for a cause requires extensive and intricate procedures. God has equipped His believers to become the representatives of His kingdom in the earth. The diplomat's responsibility is to achieve the task assigned without compromising their status or position. Moreover, the task of the believer is to serve as the highest diplomatic authority to represent God, and accomplish the cause of Christ. Every believer should view himself as the authority God has placed in the earth to accomplish His goals and purpose.

Father, As you have equipped me to be your representative, keep me covered by the Blood of Jesus. You have given me the necessary tools, therefore, I choose to use them in a proper way so that you will receive all the praise. Let me not fulfill any self-centered motives or actions which do not line up with your Word. As I walk with you, I will conduct and view myself as the true representative of God. In Jesus' Name, Amen

SECTION 3

ENDURANCE BUILDING

Day One

Romans 5:3-4, KJV

3 And not only so, but we glory in tribulations also: knowing that tribulation worketh patience; 4 And patience, experience; and experience, hope:

Spiritual endurance is the direct result of spiritual strength. When our physical bodies are strengthened we are able to physically push ourselves more. Metaphorically speaking this is how our spiritual lives should be. We experience trials and hardships which come to make our faith stronger. Stability in life is the product of great faith in Jesus Christ. As we embrace our trials our spirit receives the strength it needs for our life.

Father, Teach me to embrace the path you have for me. I know that along the path there will be times that I have to endure hardships and trials, so allow me to understand what you are doing through those experiences. Your desire is that my faith in you is rooted and grounded on the principles of your Word. So show me thy truths, that I might have strength and stability which will show me to keep my hope in you. In Jesus' Name, Amen

Day Two

Luke 24:49, KJV

49 And, behold , I send the promise of my Father upon you: but tarry ye in the city of Jerusalem, until ye be endued with power from on high.

Spiritual tenacity is the diligence to ensure that goals and progress are met. God promises the result of this tenacity is to be characterized by an ability to make things happen in our lives. The power referenced in the passage, is equivalent to rain needed to grow crops---it is necessary to make what is planted become tangible. God promises power, but we have to be tenacious in making sure we receive the power God wants to give. This comes from continually praying, fasting, and seeking God. Stay tenacious and remain, for the power shall come.

Father, I receive all that you have for me in my life. I understand there are promises you give to all of your disciples. So with this understanding, show me how to see those promises come to past in my life. Give me a greater level of diligence and tenacity to be able to watch your Word become tangible, so I can feel and touch what you have promised me. Even when my strength is weakened, allow my reserves to kick in so the promises will be obtained. In Jesus' Name, Amen

Day Three

Psalms 46:10, KJV

10 Be still, and know that I am God: I will be exalted among the heathen, I will be exalted in the earth

One of the most exciting things we have working on our side as Christians is being a child of the Lord God-Elohim. As He is the highest authority, we become the exact resemblance of this same authority when we bear His name. Believers have rights and privileges under the authority of the name of God. As he is honored in the nations and world, his offspring will be honored throughout the nations and world. We have no need to open our mouth in conflict, because the fruit of our righteousness is the authority of God. Stand still and know that God, who is your God, is working on your behalf.

Father, You are the one true source of my strength and might. I know that all glory, honor, dominion, and might belong to you. For you will be exalted above all the nations of the earth. For you are the name that is above every name, and your name is what will make all men reverence your presence. So God I thank you for the authority you have given me. Show me you will work for me and I will not have to battle any attempts of confusion. As I honor you, you will be honored continually in the earth. In Jesus' Name, Amen

Day Four

Proverbs 25:7, KJV

7 For better it is that it be said unto thee, Come up hither; than that thou shouldest be put lower in the presence of the prince whom thine eyes have seen.

Honor is given to those who have been tested, tried, and proven to have endurance to overcome any attacks against them. God's desire is to give honor to those who have withstood the tests of time. Believers have to be careful to avoid a pathway of being demoted because of our rebellion, disobedience, and pride. Self-righteousness causes vain glory to be sought by those who attempt to create a path where it was not meant to be utilized. Avoid all things which tempt you to become high-minded beyond measure with pride.

Father, I don't want to be out of your will! Allow me to remain humble in my spirit so I will be able to be exalted when it is my TIME! When the enemy tempts me to look too highly of myself, show me that area so I will not allow him to gain a foothold against me. I want to receive the honor that you give your people, and I do not want the vain glory of my flesh. Show me how to remain under your mighty hand. In Jesus' Name, Amen

Day Five

Isaiah 55:11, KJV

11 So shall my word be that goeth forth out of my mouth: it shall not return unto me void, but it shall accomplish that which I please , and it shall prosper in the thing whereto I sent it.

How great it is that we have the assurance of knowing the Word of God will always bring us to a level of prosperity! Where prosperity is mentioned, we define it not in materialistic possession only, but in the total life of a person (body, soul, and spirit). We must maintain a life built upon the Word of God, in turn the fruit (outward expression) of Christ living in us will show others we have come from Him. Each Christian must be seasoned in utilizing God's Word in their daily lives so it will produce what it was meant to produce---Life.

Father, I bless you for allowing me to gain wisdom from your word and become effective in my personal life. All things outside your purpose fail, but I have the assurance that your Word will never fail. It will continually produce the life I need it to. So God I thank you for rooting me in your Word, and I thank you in advance for prospering me in all things I set my hand to do. In Jesus' Name, Amen

Day Six

Psalms 112:7, NIV

*7 He will have no fear of bad news; his heart is steadfast,
trusting in the LORD.*

The Christian's life is rooted by trusting God, which is the foundation of our beliefs. Solomon instructs us to trust God without putting our own understanding into the equation. David speaks of a man who trusts God as one who does not fear unanticipated news. As our hearts are fixed (concretely established), we are able to identify with and overcome all undue stress from unfortunate situations. Christians should not allow any condition of fear of the unknown to overthrow their foundational belief and trust in God.

Father, In this season of my life I have to know how to trust you. I have to know that I cannot dilute the effectiveness of your plan and purpose for me by mixing false perceptions into the equation. So God, teach me how to trust you. Even in the midst of unfortunate situations and circumstances, keep my heart guarded and firmly placed in the truth of your Word. I bless you for it being done now. In Jesus' Name, Amen

Day Seven

Judges 7:3, KJV

3 Now therefore go to, proclaim in the ears of the people, saying , Whosoever is fearful and afraid, let him return and depart early from mount Gilead. And there returned of the people twenty and two thousand; and there remained ten thousand.

Timidity and fear will paralyze any person's progress. Fear grips the very nature and heart of a person, not allowing him to move in any new direction. People who allow fear and timidity to overpower them will live unfilled lives, full of questions. The commonality of fear in individuals stretches from one person to the next. Individuals have to process their fear, putting it in the proper perspective so movement and progress are always possible. Those who allow fear to overtake them will put their lives in a frozen state, leading to stagnation, a lack of progress, and lack of fulfillment.

Father, When I decided to trust you and live for you my mind was in an infancy state in the spirit. Help me to process your desires. I will not let fear of the unknown paralyze me, where I am no longer being productive in my Christian walk with you. Cover my mind with your blood. Allow your Holy Spirit to become the teacher of my spirit. The old man and mindset is gone, I now clothe myself in my new man and mindset. You have not given me a fearful spirit, and I walk with a sound mind to engage in your will and way. In Jesus' Name, Amen

Day Eight

Mark 15:34, KJV

34And at the ninth hour Jesus cried with a loud voice, saying, Eloi, Eloi, lama sabachthani? which is , being interpreted , My God, my God, why hast thou forsaken me?

During times of uncertainty it is important for us to maintain a connection to our Heavenly Father. When we experience dark times, peace of mind is critical to overcome these dark seasons. Our foundational principal should be rooted in the belief that God never leaves or abandons His people. His **omnipresence, omniscience, and omnipotence** (ever present, all-knowing, and all-powerful) gives peace of mind and serenity of heart, which builds a testimony of the grace of God for each individual life.

Father, Cover and keep me during the times my life seems dark. I know that although I may experience these times, my trust lies in your word which says you will not leave me alone. Let me know that your presence is always with me even during my dark days. So when I experience these times, they will only last for a temporary moment; but your peace and joy will be with me at all times. Lord I thank you for never leaving me alone. In Jesus' Name, Amen

Day Nine

Joshua 24:22, KJV

22 And Joshua said unto the people, Ye are witnesses against yourselves that ye have chosen you the LORD, to serve him. And they said , We are witnesses.

An outward declaration provides a person with the opportunity to hear their life's expectations. When one declares something, it provides them with the desire to be held accountable to what has been spoken. Inward thoughts and expressions do not hold the weight of accountability as outward thoughts and expressions. Why? The exposing of something brings accountability to reach the desired result, as opposed to being continuously hidden. When Christians declare something over their lives, **their faith kicks in** to hold them accountable to witness what they declared come to pass. Our declarations drive us to actually become what we say, as they are driven from our faith. A declaration based from our faith allows us to witness that very thing come to pass in our lives.

Father, This is the declaration I make over my life that I will be a vessel who will continuously serve you. No matter how it looks in this present age, I know you desire people to worship you in Spirit and Truth. I make the decree to the nations and on the housetops that I will not turn my back on you or your word. I choose you, as you have chosen me from the foundation of the world. Hold me accountable to what I declare over my own life. Let my words line up with your words. I present myself over to you. In Jesus' Name, Amen

Day Ten

Mark 11:23, 24, NIV

23 "I tell you the truth, if anyone says to this mountain, 'Go, throw yourself into the sea,' and does not doubt in his heart but believes that what he says will happen, it will be done for him. 24 Therefore I tell you, whatever you ask for in prayer, believe that you have received it, and it will be yours.

The strength and power of words can never be underestimated. There is authority in the declarations which come from the heart of a person. This authority originates from being created in the likeness of God. As believers we can speak destiny, life, death, complacency, positive or negative outcomes, poverty, or prosperity. Consistent declarations of God's truths will ensure the believer exhibits their true authority in the earth. Choose to speak life, which produces POWER!

Father, Let every word that proceeds out of my mouth be according to the declaration and authority of your word. I know that when I pray to you, you hear me; and I believe because I am connected to you that my prayers are answered. Help me to never doubt your word. Teach me how to overcome every obstacle in my life, according to your promises. I thank you for all hindrances being removed now. In Jesus' Name, Amen

SECTION 4

MATURE DEVELOPMENT

Day One

Romans 4:20, KJV

*20He staggered not at the promise of God through unbelief;
but was strong in faith, giving glory to God;*

S teadfastness in believing God's promises will ensure any believer lives a life blessing God. As tests and trails come, our faith level dictates how much we believe God's promises. In the midst of hardship it is imperative that we do not become unstable. Trusting God allows for a three-dimensional way ***(Belief, Strength, and Faith)*** to praise Him for who He is and His ability.

Father, As I continually walk with you I will not become unstable by the trials and tests I have to endure. Through those times I will allow my spirit to become stronger in the faith of your word. I know that you will not lead me into the wrong places. So even now I glorify you, knowing that I shall receive clear and greater revelation knowledge from you. In Jesus' Name, Amen

Day Two

Revelations 3:8, KJV

8I know thy works: behold, I have set before thee an open door, and no man can shut it: for thou hast a little strength, and hast kept my word, and hast not denied my name.

Access into divine areas of living is given to all believers who trust in the power and ability of God. Believers are anointed to do extraordinary feats according to their faith in God's word. An open door signifies access into divine areas with authority. When you keep God's Word, you become limitless, as God blesses and positions you for His purposes to manifest in your life.

Father, Your Word is truth and life to me. I know you watch over your word to perform it, so I will continually hold on to it. Even when my strength seems to be minimized I thank you for renewing my strength. I will never turn my back on you, as I know you will never turn your back on me. As I hold on to you, I believe and thank you for access to the promises of your Word. In Jesus' Name, Amen

Day Three

Hebrews 11:23, KJV

23 By faith Moses, when he was born , was hid three months of his parents, because they saw he was a proper child; and they were not afraid of the king's commandment.

God's people should be ready to assume their divine mantle. A mantle covers and smears a person symbolizing their power and position. Divine demonstrations of power are accomplished because of mantles. When we are aware of the position we hold, fear will never settle in. Our confidence comes from knowing we will fulfill and demonstrate God's authority in the earth.

Father, I bless you now for the position, power, and mantle that you have given me. I know that you have called me to walk in areas that I have not been before. I know that you have strengthened me to walk out of places of complacency, and into places of supernatural ability. So God, as I walk according to the mantle you have placed upon me, I thank you for the strength to subdue and overcome any words spoken contrary to this truth. I will do all to demonstrate your authority in the earth. In Jesus' Name, Amen

Day Four

Isaiah 54:14, KJV

14 In righteousness shalt thou be established : thou shalt be far from oppression; for thou shalt not fear : and from terror; for it shall not come near thee.

Righteousness produces the three-fold cord of solidification, freedom, and protection. As believers we are sustained because of our faithfulness to God's Word. Fear cannot come close especially during fearful moments. Striving to maintain a life of righteousness ensures our connection with God is not broken, and all forms of oppression will be subdued.

Father, My spirit is overjoyed because my life is grounded in You. For your keeping power allows me to become all that you have destined me to be. I thank you for the enemy being at bay, not being able to tempt or terrorize my mindset or beliefs. My beliefs are established in your word which is the foundation of righteousness. As I maintain righteousness, keep me grounded in you. In Jesus' Name, Amen

Day Five

Deuteronomy 13:4, KJV

4 Ye shall walk after the LORD your God, and fear him, and keep his commandments, and obey his voice, and ye shall serve him, and cleave unto him.

Anything revered will hold a special place in our life. As fine china is kept precious, we should keep God's word in our heart, never allowing outside contaminates to enter. When we reverence God and His word we understand His purity. When we understand His purity, our will-power pushes us to maintain a pure lifestyle. The mechanisms we use to allow this to materialize is by serving Him, being obedient, holding to Him, and reverencing Him.

Lord, You are to be reverenced above all things in the earth. You are above all situations, people, and governments; and should be reverenced as such. I hold to your word, for they will produce life in my spirit. As life is produced I will begin to flourish in every pathway you have for me. Continue to keep me in the posture of serving you, being obedient to your Word, and holding to it. As I do this I will live a life which brings glory and honor to your name. In Jesus' Name, Amen

Day Six

III John 1:12, KJV

12Demetrius hath good report of all men, and of the truth itself: yea, and we also bear record ; and ye know that our record is true.

What is the reputation the Body of Christ has amongst the world? What is the reputation individual believers have amongst the world? Our reputation is important as it signifies if we exemplify God's nature. Can people speak well of us when our name is mentioned? Our daily walk with God should produce the character of a good report. The tree is known by the fruit it produces.

Father, I need to know what my reputation is among the people I live with daily. My desire is that when people hear my name they know that my spirit coincides with your spirit. Let me not have an evil reputation. Let me have a good report and represent your name in the best way possible. As your disciples of old maintained a good report, let my life be lived so that my report shall be well spoken of by many. In Jesus Name, Amen

Day Seven

1 John 4:20-21, KJV

20 If a man say , I love God, and hateth his brother, he is a liar: for he that loveth not his brother whom he hath seen , how can he love God whom he hath not seen ? 21 And this commandment have we from him, That he who loveth God love his brother also.

Unforgiveness is cancerous to the Body of Christ. Similar to the disease, if continuing undetected it can become the demise of good people. Although naturally cancer cannot be transferred to another, the outward effects can pull others into the struggle. Things identified as hazardous need expedient removal. ***Loving God's people is a commandment not an option***. Regardless of their actions toward us, our obligation as "true" Christians is to respond out of love. True love is unconditional; God's love is not based on a prerequisite, nor does it need to be reciprocated for Him to still love us. ***As believers we cannot conditionally love others, but love others unconditionally***.

Father, Your word declares that I need to walk in love toward all people. Show me how to forgive as Christ forgives. Teach me how to be truly healed from past hurts that were caused by the mishandling of others. My desire is not to live life as a hypocrite, so show me how to love. Even when situations arise which cause me to become angry, teach me how to continually love. I do not want the cancer of unforgiveness to begin to take root in my life. Strengthen my heart, mind, and spirit to love all people as you do. In Jesus' Name, Amen

41

Day Eight

Judges 5:31, KJV

31 So let all thine enemies perish , O LORD: but let them that love him be as the sun when he goeth forth in his might. And the land had rest forty years.

R epeated victories in Christ are the result of continual strength for believers. When connected to the Father, we are capable of doing mighty exploits; which in turn defeats the enemy. When we are strengthened by God, our spirit, soul, and body can be at rest. This strength impacts those who encounter us bringing all to a level of peace and victory. As we go forth we should impact the lives of many, providing them with the necessary tools to become victorious in their life.

Father, Thank you for allowing your people to live in victory, and be strengthened by continually winning life's battles. I am confident in your ability to bring peace to any situation. As I walk in peace, let me bring peace to anyone I come in contact with. Strengthen me so the enemy will not gain an advantage over my spirit. Thank you in advance. In Jesus' Name, Amen

Day Nine

1 Kings 18:21, KJV

21 Elijah went before the people and said, "How long will you waver between two opinions? If the LORD is God, follow him; but if Baal is God, follow him." But the people said nothing.

Instability halts the progression of faith and trust in God. Moreover, if a believer in Christ is unstable, they will never mature to their full capability. As Christians our desire should be to serve God with all our inner-most being. Once we are established all other areas of our environment will follow. Why? Due to the creation of an internal culture reproducing externally.

Father, My mind is stable in knowing that I will serve you all the days of my life. Let me avoid being like the double minded man. Your desire for me is that I be established from the belief and faith in you. Once established internally all other aspects of my life will follow. Thank you God, for making me stable and well-rounded in all areas of my life. In Jesus' Name, Amen

Day Ten

Genesis 49:9-10, NIV

9 You are a lion's cub, O Judah; you return from the prey, my son. Like a lion he crouches and lies down, like a lioness--who dares to rouse him? 10 The scepter will not depart from Judah, nor the ruler's staff from between his feet, until he comes to whom it belongs and the obedience of the nations is his.

You are the called and selected of God! How great it is to recognize this selection and understand the capacity and ability you have! Your spiritual DNA is composed of ruler-ship and kingship! You carry the mantle to reign in the earth! How excellent it is to be anointed as kings, priests, and royalty in the spirit and in the earth. Walk in the authority you have, defeating sin and all manner of evil. You are seated together with Christ in Heavenly places! Reign Believer, Reign!

Father, As you have shown me who I am in you, I will walk in who you have shown me I am. You have anointed me with fire and rulership! You have decreed that my life will represent you. You have placed the authority of kingship in my spirit! I thank you because the enemy cannot prohibit me from ruling in the earth. So I will rule here until you come again and we will rule together. Thank you Lord! In Jesus' Name, Amen

Notes

Notes

Notes

Notes

Notes

The 40 Day Way

<u>Receiving Christ as Lord</u>

1. We recognize that we need a Savior because of our sinful nature.
    - Romans 3:23- For all have sinned and come short of the glory of God.
    - Romans 5:12- Wherefore, as by one man sin entered into the world, and death by sin; and so death passed upon all men, for that all have sinned

2. We understand Jesus came to be the ransom for our sins.
    - John 3:16- For God so loved the world, that he gave his only begotten Son, that whosoever believeth in him should not perish , but have everlasting life
    - Hebrews 9:28- So Christ was once offered to bear the sins of many; and unto them that look for him shall he appear the second time without sin unto salvation.

3. We receive and confess Jesus as Lord of our life.
    - Romans 10:10- For with the heart man believeth unto righteousness; and with the mouth confession is made unto salvation.

If you would like to receive Christ as Lord, pray this prayer:

Dear Lord, I come to you now acknowledging I am a sinner. I recognize I need your blood to cleanse me from all my unrighteousness. I repent of my sins and ask for your forgiveness. I receive Christ now as my Lord and Savior. In Jesus' Name, Amen.

Now that you have received Christ begin to study His word and pray continually. God bless you and keep you!

The 40 Day Way

Scriptures for life's situations

Peace
Isaiah 26:3- "Thou wilt keep him in perfect peace"
Psalms 29:11- "The Lord will bless his people with..."
Psalms 122:7- "Peace be within thy walls"

Joy
Nehemiah 8:10- "The joy of the Lord is your strength"
Isaiah 61:3- "The oil of joy for mourning...

Anger
Ephesians 4:26- " Be ye angry and sin not..."
Galatians 5:22- " But the fruit of the spirit is..."

Worry
Philippians 4:6- "Be careful for nothing..."
2 Corinthians 4:17- "For our light affliction..."
John 14:27- "Let not your heart be troubled..."

Faith
Hebrews 11:6-"And without faith it is impossible..."
James 2:18- "I will shew thee my faith..."
Hebrews 10:23- "Let us hold to the profession..."

Prayer
James 5:16- "The effectual fervent prayer..."
James 5:15- "And the prayer of faith..."
1 Thessalonians 5:17- "Pray without ceasing"
1 Timothy 2:8- "I will therefore that men pray..."

Scriptures for life's situations (continued)

Doubt

James 1:6- "But...ask in faith nothing wavering..."
James 1:8- "A double-minded man is unstable..."
Mark 11:23-"...and shall not doubt in his heart..."

Forgiveness

Mark 11:25- "And when ye stand praying, forgive..."
Matthew 5:24- "...first be reconciled to thy brother..."
Luke 17:4- "And if he trespass...thou shalt forgive..."

Sickness

Psalms 103:3- "...who healeth all thy diseases."
Matthew 10:1- "...and to heal all manner of sickness..."
Isaiah 53:5- "and with his stripes we are healed."
Jeremiah 33:6- "Behold, I will bring it health..."

Sin

Numbers 18:32- "And ye shall bear no sin..."
Romans 3:23- "For all have sinned..."
Romans 6:15- "What then? Shall we sin..."
Matthew 6:12- "And forgive us our debts..."

Lawrence L. Trimble is a minister of the gospel in Decatur, IL. As a father, motivational speaker, human services worker, and community leader, he utilizes his spiritual background when working with organizations, communities, youth groups, and families. As a professional in the community, Lawrence has a strong passion to impart the spiritual principles of Christ in every realm of influence. He has assisted many initiatives and organizations such as: Boy Scouts of America, Decatur schools truancy plan, alternative education programs, and positive behavior strategies to name a few. Lawrence has also served on various community committees for his community's common good.

Lawrence strongly believes that God's people should impact all areas they encounter whether secular or spiritual. He ministers hope with a passion through motivational speaking, preaching, mentoring, and teaching God's Word. Lawrence is father to three sons and is married to the love of his life Brittanie.

If you would like to order more copies of this book or other publications, please contact Strong Publishing House via email at strongpublishinghouse@gmail.com or visit our website at strongpublishinghouse.weebly.com

If you would like to invite Lawrence Trimble to your event, youth group, church group or event, or organization you can contact him via email at lawrencetrimble@gmail.com or
by telephone
217-519-6045, office

www.ingramcontent.com/pod-product-compliance
Lightning Source LLC
Chambersburg PA
CBHW071851020426
42331CB00007B/1949